Solid Ground

SOLID GROUND

*How I Built a 7-Figure Company at 22
with Zero Capital*

SEVETRI WILSON

Solid Ground Innovations

New Orleans, LA

Solid Ground: How I Built a 7-Figure Company at 22 with Zero Capital

ISBN-13: 978-0-578-47980-4

Published in the United States by Solid Ground Innovations, New Orleans, LA.

Author website: http://www.sevetriwilson.com

Connect: @sevetriwilson.

Author Photo: Shagari Gerard (Mosaic by MG)

Clothing: H Kyle Boutique

Hair: Ashanti Lation

Editor: Nakia J.S. Thomas (Few Editorial & Creative Suite)

CONTENTS

ACKNOWLEDGEMENTS

I can't tell you how many people have told me or asked me when I was going to write a book. I could have gone in so many different directions with my very first book, but I wanted to ensure it was geared toward business. I also didn't want the first book to be about something as mundane and network-influenced as raising capital. Instead, I chose to write about how I built my first business. It's important for me to show the journey that it took for me to get to where I am today although I still have so much more I want to do and accomplish. I hope these nuggets, secret hacks, and real-life stories help at least one.

I want to thank so many people. Thank you to Nakia for helping to edit and coach me through this thing. To my tribe of close friends, Zi, Christina, Tia, Shayla, Lyndsey, Heather and you too, Izzy. To all the men and women that inspire me that I've met and have yet to meet. To E, the Thomas Bros, Ebony, Ted, Unc Phil, Landon and Remiah for keeping my creative juices going and for believing in my brand power. To my dear friend and mental health check reminder, Summer. To Tyrus, Lane, Sharon, and Tony for giving me my first shot in four completely different arenas. To my amazing team who are superheroes in their own right. To my siblings, Schod, Shannon, Sedric, Troy, T.K. and Shante. To my sassy aunts who are like my second mothers, Aunt Emily and Aunt Diann. To my mentors and guides, Zara, Ameen, Raymond, Rod, and so many others that it would take the rest of this book to name. And finally, to my daddy and mama because even in death you continue to give me life. Thank you.

Your biggest problem of the day should be how you are going to bridge the gap between where you are and where you want to be.

– Sevetri Wilson

PREFACE

Screw it. The Forbes lists, the article features, the media and press. These things are heavily based on networks and who you know. In fact, the most successful business people I know you've probably never heard of. You know why? Because they are more concerned about making money and leaving a legacy than becoming famous.

This book isn't going to show you how to build your brand to sell thousands of products on social media. This book will instead show you how to build a "social media proof" business. One that if social media disappeared tomorrow or if your account was deactivated you wouldn't skip a beat. This isn't a book for those seeking fame. This book is for those willing to put in the work. Those willing to fix their finances and those who have the resiliency (even if you thought you didn't) to keep getting back up after rejections have knocked you down.

This book is for you.

This is how I built my first 7-figure company at 22 with no capital.

INTRODUCTION

You know how people say *just do the work and the rest will come*? Well, that's exactly what happened to me. I was behind the scenes with my head down working when countless opportunities started to open up for me. It didn't happen immediately, but when it did, it happened quickly.

But, before we dive into what happened between zero and seven figures, let's go back to before my first real business idea was even thought of, which for me was right after college.

At the start of 2009, I was a 22-year-old graduate student with big plans for using my degrees in mass communication and history. Let me tell you, I just *knew* I was going to become a professor, make documentary films, and be a true historian. One of my professors was such a great influence in my life that I wanted to influence other students in the same way. Yet, I knew I was always an entrepreneur. It was just who I was. From the first time I launched my first idea, an online website called *B-Now*, to where I am today.

Right after college, I was also working for a nonprofit called CASA (Court Appointed Special Advocates). This is where my love for philanthropy and the community became more dominant in my life. There I was responsible for putting together programs and other campaigns to see through the mission of the organization. From this work, I began to receive inbound requests to help others on their projects. (*See what I mean about doing the work and people noticing?*) Then, a friend of mine who was playing professional sports reached out to me and asked if I could help him start a nonprofit. My initial reaction was *no, I have a job*, and at first, I didn't think it was a real opportunity.

After much consideration, I finally agreed to come on board and create what became the Tyrus Thomas Foundation. Tyrus was playing sports in Chicago at the time and had an immense desire to help the youth in the city of Chicago as well as in his hometown of Baton Rouge. After doing my own analysis of what would be needed, I committed to this position full-time and quickly journeyed into making a difference through the world of sports philanthropy.

My work received a number of great accolades, including being honored with a Nobel Prize for public service, the Jefferson Award, and recognition in the White House report to the U.S. Senate on volunteerism in U.S. People wondered, "Who's behind the scenes of the Tyrus Thomas Foundation? Who's doing this?"

Quite naturally, my reputation grew and so did my referrals. People were interested in me helping them build their programs and curriculums from the ground up. As consultancy work started to come in, I knew I needed to get serious about taking the appropriate measures to build my own team to handle the workload. I felt there was an opportunity here for me to utilize the momentum and start an official consultancy company. So, I did what everyone does; I filed for my LLC and birthed my first company, Solid Ground Innovations, in 2009. I would go on to work with other athletes such as Lolo Jones and Warrick Dunn and over a dozen others.

> *Side note to my up and coming entrepre-*
> *neurs: When you file for an LLC (Legal Liability*
> *Company), get your mind properly wrapped*
> *around taxes, what's needed to maintain the*
> *reports for that company, and the requirements*
> *for handling the money you'll be receiving.*

I took almost two years to ensure I had my affairs in order with starting a business. I didn't file papers and announce it to the world the next day. In fact, I'm a believer of moving in silence until you really get things going for yourself. By 2011, I had officially stepped out of my comfort zone, launched my business to the public, and began consulting full-time. Although I'd always had an entrepreneurial spirit, I hadn't dreamed of doing what I'm doing today.

I am writing this book in an effort to show you how to avoid some of the same mistakes I made through this journey. I hope to show you that I didn't just step into this. This didn't happen overnight. It took me three years to really get my company off the ground and get a solid founda-tion of what my team and I were doing. Within five years, we really hit our stride, and we have been evolving ever since.

It's going to be hard. It's going to take a lot of work and sacrifice to accomplish the goals you set for yourself. It will be nothing like you imagined but could be more than you could have ever imagined, and that's why you have to keep going.

CHAPTER 1.

SOCIAL MEDIA PROOF

So, here's the thing: I got my contacts and con-tracts early on out of the dirt! When I started col-lege, social media was just beginning to be "a thing." It was definitely *not* a place for doing busi-ness as usual, at least not early on. It was where we went to show the after highlights of our day — not to market or sell anything. In fact, most of us were on Facebook without a face. We'd capture parts of our workday, which ended up building commu-nity in the long run, but in the early days, it wasn't designed to get us clients.

With that being said, the old-school way (i.e., phone calls, emails, meetings, and shaking hands) is how I built my business. Social media just became a platform to showcase my work and to deepen connections. It became an extension and another tool in the arsenal of many other tools I had collected and mastered as my personal and company's set of capabilities. Today, it's easy to land clients, promote services, and sell products over social media, but listen, if it all disappeared tomorrow, (let me be real here) our company will still be running! The solid foundation I've built within my business won't disappear with it. I'll still be in business.

Are you preparing your idea, business, or concept for the long haul?

That's what you must stop and ask yourself, especially if you have built your business on the waves of likes, follows, and reposts. It's so important for you to make your company social media proof. Of course, it's great to show what you're doing and get paid for it, but to be frank, unless you've created a long-term strategy, it's really just a short-term hustle. I'm talking about building a sustainable multimillion-dollar business here. This means building authentic relationships with people outside of social media. This means utilizing your network for what it is — social capital.

Let's say your revenue is consumer-based, solely

online, and that's all you ever want it to be — that's fine. However, make sure you know what your exit plan looks like if anything was to happen. Trust me, anything can happen. A friend of mine had a company that was social-media driven, but when Instagram made a change in their policy, it put his business in conflict with their terms. In other words, they said, *Stop doing this or we're going to shut you down.* We call that sending a cease and desist. Thankfully, his company was able to keep going off of social media, but other companies like his started to shut down.

Can you imagine the type of anxiety that comes along with a threat to delete your entire page and stop operating your company? What do you do when they say they're going to shut you down tomorrow and all of your income and followers will go with it? How would you feel knowing that all of your business posts are disappearing the next day and you're not getting them back? For an online, social-media driven business, that's mental turmoil right there. Yet, that's a reality for someone. It's still happening on social media today.

If you remember the story of what happened to @fashionbombdaily's Instagram page, you know that this is not a joke. The owner had over a million followers and on her biggest selling night of the year, they took her page down. Straight up, deleted it. In five seconds, they had completely disrupted her income and livelihood. After an entire year, she finally got it back. Since, she has talked publicly about how hard it was for her, being that Instagram was her largest revenue stream. When you're gone for that long, it's inevitable that new faces and pages will appear to take your spot, and even after you come back (*if you ever do*) it's extremely hard to rebuild. Consumers get bored easy, and they move on quickly.

None of this seems fair (*and it's not*), but it's life. Relying on social media to push your product can be a tricky and tough game to play. You should definitely capitalize on it while you can but always have another goal on the table that stretches you beyond it. For instance, how can you utilize the money you've generated online to build or invest in something else? What is your social media proof plan?

Laying out this type of blueprint for the future of your business can be one of the most important steps you make in this journey.

The hardest and yet easiest thing you'll ever do is show up even when you don't want to.

CHAPTER 2.

SHOW UP & FOLLOW UP

_____

Although I started my company in 2009, it wasn't until around 2011 or so that I really caught my stride. As a company, we had started to pivot toward doing more public and private sector work, which was influenced by mentors and individuals I met along the way. By 2014, we had phased nearly all of our original clients, professional athletes, out of our business model. (Many questioned why I made that decision, but that's a story for another day. So, I'll save you the details for now.) One key moment that first influenced this change was attending a business seminar put on by my sorority.

There were roughly 700 women in the room. John Matthews Jr., the Louisiana Economic

Development (LED) Executive Director of Small Business Services at the time, was one of the speakers. He gave us insight on how to grow a business, as well as the resources and free consultancy service his office offered. As he wrapped up, he mentioned something that stuck with me.

"I've given you all this information," he said, "but I probably won't see any of you again. When I go back to my office on Monday, no one is going to follow up with me. Hundreds, thousands of people I've spoken to and maybe one or two of them have followed up."

I thought, *Word? Bet.*

I reached out to him a week later. When I got to his office, he said, "You're the only person out of everyone at the seminar to follow up with me." I was 1 out of almost 700 women! I stood out by simply taking the initiative to follow up. That's what you must learn to do. I showed up for the business seminar, and then I followed up with the speaker on his offer to help.

Ever since then, he's been a mentor of mine, and he has continued to help me access and understand the resources that were available to me. And that's not it. A year or so later there was an opportunity in his office for work and we ended up landing the contract. This is why taking extra steps to build relationships are so important. I had found a mentor, resources, and a contract all in two steps: showing up and following up.

It's all about repeatable, consistent efforts for long periods of time. Be consistent, despite failure, and continue to keep pushing forward even if you have to take several L's along the way. Over the years, my team and I have lost *a lot* of contracts. Honestly, it took us a while to start winning them at all. I put up a considerable amount of my own money and energy, and technically, I was losing. At any point, I could have given up and went back to a regular job, but my determination and passion wouldn't allow me.

In my mind, I had already formulated what I wanted my world to look like when it came to how I made money. I was determined to be a business owner and passionate about employing people — especially people who looked like me — and building a platform for them to do what they love. That's what pushed me to continue moving forward.

The difference between me and a lot of people is I want to be wealthy and respected while others want to be superficially rich and famous.

CHAPTER 3.

MENTOR PICK-UP LINES

Over a cup of coffee one morning, a friend of mine mentioned someone of influence who he knew and thought I should connect with. (It was one of those situations where your friend doesn't "really" have enough weight to actually introduce you to that person of influence, but they thought to mention it anyway.) Naturally, if you name drop someone to me and I believe there could be a good connection there, I'm going to try to find that person on my own. So, later that night, I turned to Google. My search brought up his email address on a presentation he'd done three years prior, and from there, I was able to message him cold. Surprisingly, instead of ignoring my bold effort to connect, he acknowledged it. "I don't know how you got past my gatekeepers," he said, "but the fact that you did, means we should probably meet."

Here's a quick hack: If someone's email is out there online somewhere, you can type in that person's first name, "@", space, and then their company name, and Google retrieves it for you.

Fast forward to today, he's not only one of my advisors for my latest venture a tech startup but he's also a close mentor of mine. And here's the thing: I never had to *ask* him to be my mentor. Had I emailed him with the note *Can you be my mentor?* it would've been a recipe for disaster, and my email would have likely been ignored. Instead, I asked for a few minutes of his time to gain some insight, and once we met, my ask was simple, "Can you be a guide for me as I navigate this new chapter of my career?" Our relationship grew organically from there. I can now easily schedule time to sit with him for a chat every quarter.

People are more susceptible to sharing information than agreeing to mentorship. You know why? Because mentorship is such a heavy ask. Most people don't realize just how heavy it is. It's like asking someone for tickets to a Beyoncé concert. It's *a lot* to ask for — especially if you just met them five minutes ago. So, please, don't send a first-time email or direct message asking someone to mentor you. Your chance of getting a response is highly unlikely.

Particularly if you're grown (over the age of 18), understand that asking someone to be your mentor requires a little more thoughtfulness behind it. Sure, you may like what someone is doing and what they've achieved, but if you don't understand how to finesse your approach altogether, it's best to simply observe from afar.

Here are what I like to call "mentor pick-up lines" that you can use to get what you want *without* directly asking for mentorship:

- "Can you be a guide for me in a certain area?"

- "Do you mind giving me 30 minutes of your time? I would love to get your insight on something."

- Start by mentioning a few things you can connect with them on. For instance, fill in the blanks to lines such as: "I heard you speak at [blank] conference." Or, "I listened to your interview on [blank] podcast, and I connected to what you said about [blank]. I would love to have 30 minutes of your time."

- "I recently read your [blog/book/article], and in it you mention [blank]. I would love to have a few minutes of your time to garner insight on [blank], and I also had about 3 follow-up questions from what I read."

In most cases, if you go to the meeting prepared for what those 30 minutes will cover and you two make a connection, that person will more than likely be willing to engage with you again. Over time, this person will begin to consider you a mentee.

Let mentorships happen organically!

Personally, I am very tuned in to mentorship. I believe in it 100%. The things that I've learned from my mentors have helped me tremendously, from how to file an LLC and ensure my accounting processes are right to how to scale and connect all the dots needed to generate growth.

Another aspect to understand is that mentorship is not only for business. I have a mentor who's purely there for a breath of fresh air. There's nothing like having someone around who's going to keep it real with you and check up on you to see how you're doing. I have a collection of mentors who offer me something different for every part of my life, but I don't necessarily call them all "mentors." The relationship is just understood.

PEER MENTORSHIP

Having a strong circle of peers in your tribe is just as helpful. Don't only have friends who are around to merely hang out and have fun; have friends who will challenge your thoughts and discuss your goals with you. For instance, a group of friends and I went to Mexico at the end of last year, and we spent time creating vision boards in our hotel room.

That's peer mentorship!

I have one friend in particular who owns a boutique, and she and I talk on a regular basis about business. We share best practices, new books, new resources, and more. We keep each other accountable, and thus, have developed a peer mentorship.

Now, a major issue can arise for someone who has peer mentors but nothing above that. Meaning, they don't have relationships with people who have "been there and done that" in their field. In that case, this person will hit a ceiling and feel as if they've outgrown their circle.

Going back to the importance of building relationships: if you reach a ceiling, meaning your circle can no longer bring you the resources that you need to grow, then it's time to start networking *up*. When you're networking with your peers, you're networking across, but to access another level, you must network up.

Seek growth and life will no doubt reflect your search.

CHAPTER 4.

GET USED TO POLITICKING

If you want to hit the ground running, get through some high-profile doors, find your seat at the most unlikely tables, and maybe even find help in some seemingly unlikely places, reach out to those individuals who are technically supposed to give you a few minutes of their time. I'm talking about city council members, state representatives, and other elected officials.

What many entrepreneurs and business owners aren't aware of is that their city and state leaders have specific office hours set up to meet with constituents. Setting up these types of meetings matter because you may be struggling for months (or even years) trying to get ahold of a busy business professional. You usually can't reach them because

1) they don't have to respond to you, 2) they probably get a ton of emails, and/or 3) they have gatekeepers.

On the other hand, city council members and state reps have to be more accessible in order to cater to the needs of their voters. It's basically a part of their job descriptions. Therefore, use this free power as a weapon to grow your company. Politicians will always know the movers and shakers of their communities because that's how they raise money and get elected. You can count on their connections running deep.

When I first started my company, reaching out to my state rep and city council member was a secret power move of mine. They had no idea who I was, but I still asked to meet with them. I explained what I was trying to accomplish with my business, and without hesitation, they began to unleash an abundance of advice, a number of resources, and a list of people they wanted to connect me with. You see, I brought myself into a room that had to hear me; I had thought through what I wanted to say and what I specifically needed from the conversations, and the rest was history. Keep in mind that some of these meetings won't garner immediate returns, but it's about cultivating relationships and building your network.

You may be thinking, *Oh, I'm not political.* Well listen, you don't have to "be political." Business is political. All of it. And at the end of the day, we're all politicking our way to the next level, anyway. Get used to it!

Honestly, these types of moves are about more than just starting a business. This is important if you want to open up opportunities in *any* space. Even if you're looking for a better job, you want to get in on this. This is how you get in the right doors.

I remember a time when someone mentioned that their cousin applied for a 6-figure salary position, and my first reaction was, "Who does he know there?"

"He doesn't know anybody," she said.

The likelihood that this position had not already been promised to someone is rare! Do you really think someone is about to release a 6-figure position and there won't be a number of individuals who someone within the company knew lined up to apply for the job? It's very rare that you find that to be the case.

This type of practice in business can leave a lot of people jaded. For a second, I found myself a little jaded by it as well. But, the faster you realize how this works, the faster you can stop the pity party and learn to work smart.

Then, you'll understand how important it is to get out there and meet people, shake hands, secure relationships, get to know the leaders of your communities and get to politicking. This is how business is done.

Don't worry about someone stealing your idea. Most people don't even execute on their own ideas.

CHAPTER 5.

FIND THE GEMS

Research opens opportunities that the average business owner will never go beyond. Therefore, do... your... research! I can't stress this enough. There are a number of hidden gems out there, specifically built to help entrepreneurs get their feet off the ground, but you have to be willing to search for them.

One resource gem I found early on was located in my state economic development program. Generally, resources are hidden there for new business owners. Let's say you need to hire a firm for marketing services but don't have the money to cover the full upfront costs, you can (in most cases) turn to your economic development office and get 50% of your marketing costs taken care of. Regardless of where you reside, you can find the same or similar benefits provided by your state economic development programs for small and emerging businesses.

Another hidden gem that many entrepreneurs are unaware of is the power of becoming certified in various spaces. It gets you on "the list." For instance, if you are a minority business owner, there are certifications such as DBE (Disadvantaged Business Enterprise). This certification gets you on a list where businesses that are being incentivized or required look to contract out DBEs (i.e., woman-owned businesses, Black-owned businesses, or minority suppliers in general). This list is very short, making the opportunity advantage even greater for you. And that's not it. It's free! It costs you absolutely nothing to become certified and be listed. There are also other certifications, such as the Federal (8A) Certification. You would be doing yourself a disservice to not fully research the specs of this opportunity and start making the proper moves in that direction if you qualify.

Here's a third gem takeaway: If you're thinking about bringing on board your first person to help execute work (whether a virtual assistant, someone who helps you prepare proposals, someone who designs, writes, or whatever you need), be sure to find a generalist. A generalist is someone who's good at doing a little bit of everything.

There is no right way to find this person. You can put out a job ad, search for them on Upwork, or even approach an old friend or a family member you believe can handle the work. Overall, the main key here is to ensure the first person on your team has a very broad range of skills. Entrepreneurs can often mistakenly think that every need in the office calls for an expert that specializes in *one* set of skills, but early on, we're all trying to figure it out. So, just find really smart people and empower them to help you figure it out.

When I launched my business to the public, back in 2011, I brought on my first person — my generalist. How did I do this so early? I took some of the consultancy money I made before becoming a full-time entrepreneur and reinvested it. I would pay my generalist more than I paid myself early on because I *needed* them there, and because I had put myself in a position to be able to afford to for a while until things were moving. When you're trying to build something that requires people and you don't have the capital, that's how it works. And with a generalist, you can save time, money, and the headache of searching for a different person to handle every need that comes through the door. This person's ability alone is a hidden gem you want to be sure to uncover early on.

I used to let things weigh on me for weeks and months. Now I take a few minutes, sleep on it at most and make a decision.

CHAPTER 6.

NEW PATH, NEW EDGE

Would you know if it was time for your business to break out of one area and move into another? If not, you should. Being in tune with your capabilities and the direction of your business is key to your success in the long run.

The first version of my business was centered around nonprofit management consulting, due to my work history in that field. We focused on helping foundations connect to their philosophic missions, developing their programs, outreach, PR, branding, events, and everything else around that. But, as my company began to show consistent growth, my mind shifted toward a different direction.

This is not what I want to do forever. I thought,

analyzing my vision in its entirety. I didn't just want to offer nonprofit development and events. (By the way, I absolutely *hated* producing events. The first chance I got to completely get rid of events from my company, I did! Events are *not* and will never be my thing, and I'm OK with that.) At some point, you'll have to look at your company and vision the same way. You'll have to come to grips with whether you're doing something just to get a contract or because you truly enjoy it.

Figure out what you *really* love to do, first. Sometimes, it's as simple as doing something hands-on to find out if you love it or not. For me, although I loved working in the community with nonprofits, there was so much more I wanted to do and so much more I was *capable* of doing. For instance, I truly loved and enjoyed working in policy, so that was an area I knew I wanted to move toward. I had to fight the challenge of being locked into one space because ultimately, it wasn't the only thing I was good at. I would go on to find another way to help the nonprofit sector, and if you are familiar with my story then you probably already know what that is. Again, another story for another day.

But, along this journey, I took the time to figure out our next direction, which eventually opened up a new path and a new challenge — securing contracts with public and private sectors. I began to strategically redesign what my business looked like, in hopes of breaking out of the nonprofit world and gaining business with other types of clients. I built a new outlook for the company and changed our focus from nonprofit management consulting to strategic communications and management. This decision also changed the dynamic of what our proposals needed to look like in order to bring in the clients I wanted to attract. (*We'll get into quality standards for proposals in chapter 11.*)

It's never going to feel all the way right. You're not always going to be comfortable with your choice. On this journey, you're going to have to have faith and through trials be able to keep it.

CHAPTER 7.

CATCH THE STRATEGY VIBE

Sometimes, the best strategy tactic starts with a mere vibe. It's when you have a good feeling about a certain approach, catch on to what's needed, and then watch things align. That's how it happened for us.

As our company services changed, we searched for ways to branch out, and there was one area in particular that grabbed our attention the most. Law firms. Besides the few attorneys we saw on billboards every day, there were tons doing business under the radar, still trying to figure out the best practices for their marketing and branding. Once we recognized this point of opportunity, we went with it.

First, we made a list of the key law firms in our

community that we could get in front of and build relationships with. Then, we created tailored proposals to meet their needs. From there, we set up meetings with their executives, laid out our capabilities, and presented exactly what we were offering. We'd oversee the rebuilding of their websites, visual marketing, branding — you name it. With a unique package, specific to their industry, on the table, we were able to land a number of contracts.

We had officially caught the strategy vibe for the season we were in, and things started to align organically. We had created a bell funnel of clientele and a funnel of recurring revenue.

CONSUMER MARKETING VS. RECURRING REVENUE

When you're first starting, all you need are a few solid customers, right? Well, that's only true if they're generating recurring revenue for you. That's not the case with consumer marketing. Consumer marketing consists of selling to a new customer every day. With that method, you're likely to end up bringing in one-time revenue with most customers. However, recurring revenue is when you're getting checks every month, signing yearly contracts, and able to count on money coming through the door on a more consistent basis.

Recurring revenue has always been and will always be the goal for me and my business models. *That's* where you want to be. That's the key. Consumer marketing is hard — trying to lock-in a new, loyal customer daily, usually through social media, can be difficult! But, turning their service into recurring revenue makes all the difference.

How do you get to recurring revenue? Start by studying your answer to this question: "Who do you want your client to be?" That's essential. A large part of constructing good strategy is choosing exactly who you want to sell to.

Let's say you want to be in the hospitality space and offer concierge services or marketing and branding to hotels. First, create a signature service for that group and deliver nothing less than high-quality products to them. Turn them into recurring revenue. If you knock out one sector really well, it allows you to open up and move into other spaces. I didn't concentrate *everything* on lawyers, but lawyers were an easy customer base for us to knock out of the park. It was also somewhat of a turnkey solution because all of their services were pretty similar.

So, while recurring revenue came through from that end, I was going after private contracts and other high-profile opportunities as well.

You start a business to make money. Period. Any-thing else is just a passion project.

CHAPTER 8.

THINK PROFIT

One of the biggest problems I see entrepreneurs run into is their process in trying to finance their business or attain the capital they need to get their business off the ground. Businesses often times, especially early on, don't have a consistent stream of revenue. We often hear about people's gross revenue but not their net profits (which is the actual profit after working expenses not included in the calculation of gross profit). Starting a business can be very volatile on your finances. If you are already in a not so good financial position, starting a business can sometimes make it worse. As best as you can, get your personal finances in order *before* starting a business.

Depending on the type of business you are

starting, it can require you to purchase items such as inventory or pay consultants or employees to execute work for the business itself. Often times, when your business is new and doesn't have its own financial history, banks will look at your personal credit score. I've seen many entrepreneurs wreak havoc on their personal credit score because they were trying to conserve money to pay employees or take care of other business-related expenses. In doing this, they may have neglected their own personal finances — (i.e. paying student loans back late or skipping a mortgage payment, etc.) All of which can wreck your personal credit, making it impossible to get a loan for your business or other business needs when you have to give a personal guarantee.

It's important to understand your *cost* of doing business. What are the upfront costs going to be before you get the business off the ground? What can you anticipate your monthly costs being? Here are a couple of pointers to keep in mind:

- Save your money. It can be really tempting to "treat yourself" with that new purse or shoes if you have a good month, but as a business owner, you have to plan for the long run.

- Don't spend money that isn't yours just because it's in your bank account. Whatever you do, keep your personal finances *separate* from your business finances, and keep your vendor money and the money you need to pay monthly expenses separate from your profits. There are many financial app tools out there, like QuickBooks, for small businesses. Hire a good accountant and not the one who is going to try and cover your tracks and hide money. (*Y'all already know what I'm talking about.*)

Ultimately, if you are not financially prepared to start a business, you may want to ease into this lifestyle by starting it as a side gig until you have generated income. It's important to be aware of the volatility of a business and its effects on your personal finances.

UNDERSTAND WEALTH CREATION

The idea of the broke entrepreneur is real. We must figure out how to create more profitable businesses. I see the numbers all the time, especially for Black women. They say that we are the fastest growing group amongst new business owners. Yet, none of that matters if you aren't making money, or even worse if you are losing money. Whether you want to build a large corporation with a number of employees or a lifestyle business from home, it doesn't matter. I have friends and family members who couldn't imagine doing what I do. They'd rather work from their homes in their slippers. And that's cool, too! Both are opportunities. The point is to understand the depths of your *own* dreams, and then figure out how to make it profitable.

Everyone's path is different. What's your path? What are you looking to do? If you're building a lifestyle business, you'll eventually have to decide if you're open to having a full staff one day. A corporation with 10 or more employees may not be what you signed up for. You may want to stay small, save, and invest your money. Investing is also an option for those working a regular 9-5 job. For instance, my brother has a normal job and invests his money in stocks and markets. He doesn't want to be an entrepreneur. *Y'all can have that life*! he says. And I get it. He has no desire for this entrepreneur lifestyle, and he doesn't have to.

Don't let these get-rich entrepreneur stories fool you. Don't allow the system to sell you the entrepreneurship dream and have you assuming this is the *only* way to create wealth. There are countless people in corporate America getting paid, too! They're setting themselves up for a nice life, where they can have money to pass down to their kids.

Regardless of the side of business you're standing on (whether employer or employee), it's not about looking busy. It's about figuring out how to profit and generate wealth.

When pricing your services, the first thing you're going to have to come to grips with is if you want your services to be perceived as economical — or exceptional?

CHAPTER 9.

GET THE PRICE RIGHT

How to price your services is one of the things I get asked often. It's also one of the most important things you will do when starting a business. It can vary from service to service. Generally, there are three models that most people follow: cost-based pricing, market-based pricing, and value-based pricing.

Cost-based pricing was one of the first models I learned of when starting my business. It essentially looks at the price based on what it costs you to "do business." On the other hand, market-based pricing takes into consideration what other people are charging.

With market-based pricing, you must be careful not to fall into what I like to call an "upside down contract," where you're losing money versus making money. New entrepreneurs can be lured to reduce their prices so that they can "compete," and early on, this is something you must consider. What are other people charging in your field? Can you compete? What is your market's tolerance for your prices? Whether you are charging for an event, pricing clothing, or consulting, you will need to get a feel for what your market will tolerate and pay.

Then, there's value-based pricing to consider. This concept puts the client in the driver's seat and allows him or her to set the value of your goods or services. This route begins whenever you ask the question, "What's your budget for X?" The response is going to be based on the value assigned by the customer, and at that point, you will have to make a decision. Does the budget work for you? Or, are you underpricing yourself, and leaning toward a rate that is not cost-based and not profitable? That's what you don't want to do. When entrepreneurs and business owners tell me that a potential client "doesn't have a budget" and it's difficult to figure out how much leeway they can have with pricing, I always respond the same way. "No such thing!" I point out. *"Every-one* has a budget because everyone has a price that they wouldn't pay."

Understanding the dynamics of how to price your services is so important. If you are working from a clean slate, the standard calculation for pricing is to take whatever your base hourly rate is, estimate the hours the project will take you, multiply your hourly rate by the number of hours to work, and then add padding. There are some people out there who will charge for minimal things, like 20 minutes for checking email. Personally, that's not my style. It looks as if you're pinching for pennies, which in my own experience is annoying. Instead, what you can do is add padding, it allows you to include the overall price of communication (i.e. emails, meetings, and calls) into your price.

Ensure your prices are clear and be confident that you can deliver the service the client is requesting, which validates your value. I have a friend who's so knowledgeable about what she does that she's able to offer a premium product for a couple of thousands of dollars. Someone may be trying to do the same thing but offering it at $199.

The difference between those two is that she's an expert, through and through, in what she's doing. She feels *more than* validated to offer it at that rate, and because she's able to get that across, people buy it.

You should understand that just because you start at one price that doesn't mean you have to stay there. When I first started, I was charging $75 per hour for my consultancy services, and today, I charge $250. Some of my mentors charge $400 and up. Once you become comfortable in charging and pricing your work, don't *stay* comfortable. It's OK to increase your prices over time. Has your delivery of service improved? Are you able to offer a better product now than before? Have you increased efficiencies? All of that matters. You can also align your higher rate by considering how much experience you have and if you are highly sought out. All of those things may allow you to inflate your price. In the end, you want to look at your capabilities and the timeframe in which you're delivering something and base the reasoning behind your price on that.

First and foremost, ask yourself, "What do I need to make? What do I need to charge to be profitable?" Regardless of the type of business you're in, you have to figure out how much it's going to cost you to do what you do. Evaluate your bandwidth. Calculate what you'll need to execute the project in its entirety. You'll have to consider your material, resources, overhead, and labor costs, as well as factor in *your time*. And then, conclude what you want to make over that to make a profit. If you don't look at your profit margins and understand what that looks like, you'll end up hustling backward. For instance, let's say you charge $125 for a service and you have to pay someone $50 to design it and another person $50 to proofread it — what's left? Looking at the profit, was it worth your time? If it wasn't, raise your rates. You were meant to run forward, not backward.

Trust me, the backward hustle is not a business.

At some point, you have to understand what you're worth and the value in which you're pricing your services. I suggest pricing higher than you normally think you should. Most times, when starting a business, people are quick to underprice because they feel as if they haven't been doing it long enough. This is understandable, but I must emphasize that you still *do not* want to undercharge. You will come to resent the project and work involved if you do this too many times. You're in business to make money and anything that doesn't is a passion project.

It all boils down to understanding your profit possibility number. That's where a lot of business owners mess up when they look at their growth. They'll say something like, *I made a million dollars this year*. But what they really mean to say is that they *grossed* a million dollars this year. You must ask yourself questions that lead back to your possibility number, such as how much do you want to *net* this upcoming year? What is your goal in real dollars in the bank? From there, you'll be on the right track to determining the right price for your market and overall company outlook.

As much as we'd like to believe the clock resets, it doesn't. Every day is just a continuation of the last. One key thing in this journey is you're going to have to let go and forgive yourself for mistakes.

CHAPTER 10.

FEARLESS PAPERWORK

Your reputation is all that you have. For this reason, delivering quality work is key. Of course, you're not going to be perfect. You're going to have some things fall through the cracks. There are going to be things you could've done better. Someone on your team may have dropped the ball — maybe, you dropped the ball. Things happen. That's business. All in all, the quality of work you deliver should have a foundation of consistency — not just in words and actions but *also* on paper.

While running a business, you may run into people who try to trap you. This is why setting your prices right and having your paperwork together are so important. Let's say you're doing an event and you only charge x-amount of money, but you also have to hire people. If you didn't budget properly this will cause you to go into a deficit, making it hard for you to actually perform and produce a quality job — all because you didn't set your price right. No one is happy in that situation. Not you, not anyone.

Today, I'm in a position where I can turn down work — if I can't do what I need to with what someone is trying to give me. If I can't pay my team *and* deliver it with the quality they're looking for, I can't take it on. On the other hand, I also know when an opportunity is worth bending on and when it's not. You must know the difference! If you're not careful, people can set you up for failure.

Ensure you set expectations, right from the beginning, so that both you and the client can clearly see what is expected for the project. You never want to over deliver on something that wasn't included in the scope of work. Entrepreneurs can easily find themselves falling into that. (*It has definitely happened to me before.*)

Documentation can't be ignored or skipped in the process of doing business. Keep *everything* written down. I remember doing a launch for a restaurant years ago, and when we first gave them the proposal for what they wanted and what it costs, they said their budget was smaller than what the proposal called for.

"Okay," I responded respectfully. "Well, for your budget, we propose something else."

Apparently, the person we were talking to didn't translate the changes to their other silent owners, so when we delivered, this person was upset! They came at me with, "Your team didn't do this. Your team didn't do *that*."

"Ma'am," I calmly replied back, pointing fearlessly at our paperwork. "You didn't pay for that. You paid for *this*."

They ended up coming back and apologizing. But the lesson here is to be aware that those types of people are out there and would try to slander your name and say you didn't do your job. Again, this is why you must keep track of things on paper to avoid getting caught in the tangles of a misconstrued business deal. Don't be afraid to say, "No ma'am. Read." It's fundamental.

Another thing: don't be afraid of someone who says they're going to sue you. Let me tell you, that's a scare tactic in the business world. The first time someone said they might sue me, I was shook. Literally. I was so nervous. Then, I found out that lawsuit threats are often times just a part of doing business. If you try that on me today, I'd sit back calmly and say, "Sue me. If you *really* want to sue me."

You have to be fearless in business, and you have to build the team around you to be just as fearless. Let nothing shake you.

Accountability is harder than a mug. But, some of the things going wrong, that's on you.

CHAPTER 11.

WIN THE BID WAR

The first proposal we put out sucked. The worst part about it? We had no idea. No one could tell us it wasn't everything that it was supposed to be. On top of that, we'd taken an extremely long time to prepare all three parts of it, so we *really* thought we had something special.

There we were, expecting to win big, going after a sizable public-sector contract worth hundreds of thousands of dollars (close to 1.8 million over 3 years), not knowing we were nowhere close to beating out the competition.

When we received our feedback, we were seriously upset (even started to blame "the man" for not accepting us). However, there happened to be an upside to it all. Someone who was an insider allowed us to review the winning proposal, and when we did, we had to agree on accepting this one thing for sure: *Our proposal really did suck*!

It was such a great lesson to learn early on. Why? Because sometimes, we think it's *them* and not us. When in actuality, it really is *us*. "The man" wasn't holding us back this time. The L was totally our fault. Although we had a capable team, we hadn't effectively demonstrated via our proposal that we could do the work that it would take. We needed to up our proposal game — and admitting that was the first step to conquering it.

Those experiences allowed us to become stronger and understand what kind of capabilities we needed as a company. We also saw the benefits of adding independent contractors into our proposals in order to help our team appear stronger. This is definitely an important hack to keep in mind. If you see someone that would be a strong addition to a proposal you're bidding for, reach out to that person and ask to include their information as a part of your team. Not only will you be increasing the quality of your proposal, but you'll also be establishing capabilities of producing an impeccable product. Also, you don't have to pay those individuals unless you win the project.

JUMP ON THE PARTNERSHIP WAGON

One hack that I wish I'd learned much sooner was the tactic of reaching out to business owners who *already* have major contracts. Majority of the time, people are subcontracting their work out to other firms. They're not doing all of that work in-house, which creates a great opportunity for you.

If you can create a relationship with a company who will give you a contract to subcontract underneath their company, then you are reducing the work you would've had to do in order to secure a contract on your own. You end up skipping the long and in-depth process of preparing for the contract. In a partnership, all you'd have to do is show up with your capabilities and have the capacity to do the work. That's it. In essence, you should see that a partnership proposal win is still a win for you. It will also help you understand what it takes to go after larger contracts on your own.

When you're working this hard and have been working this long, sometimes you forget what success looks like.

CHAPTER 12.

LAND THE ANCHOR CLIENT

The game changer for my company came after only three years of launching to the public when we picked up Aetna Better Health and CC's Coffee House as clients. (*This is where relationship building and researching certification lists come into play as I mentioned in chapter 5.*)

Aetna Better Health was looking to expand its Medicaid program to Louisiana. They turned to Louisiana's Hudson Initiative, a certification program that is designed to help eligible Louisiana small businesses gain greater access to purchasing and contracting opportunities that are available at the State government level. (*We had found this gem a while back and was on the list.*) Aetna's team searched for businesses that were consumer-driven and had a deep connection in the community.

They saw our company listed, visited our website, and then requested that we submit a proposal. Out of all the other companies they reached out to, our company ended up being selected to do their marketing statewide. This was a multimillion-dollar contract alone, and we weren't even the most prominent company on the list. What helped us get through the door was our connection to the people in the city. Our company was grounded in the community, and there wasn't another company, regardless of size, that could come to the table with the local network and community trust we had.

Nowadays, companies are looking to go beyond billboards and radio to market their brand; they're trying to get close to their constituents. They want to create better connections with the people on the ground. Thus, knowing the community well became an advantage of ours. It was ironic to see, as this was where we came from — working with nonprofits and the people of our community. It all tied back to where we started. This goes to show you that just because you don't enjoy doing something today, doesn't mean it can't be used as a tool to direct you in an area you're moving into tomorrow.

Now we had Aetna on our resume. Landing a contract with them changed the game for us in several ways. We were now working with a Fortune 100 company. We were able to add more bandwidth to our company and several more team members to support the work. Not to mention, it made us better, overall; we were now savvier in branding and marketing. You see, we couldn't go and create what we thought looked good. We had to go through their branding workshop, where we were trained on how to use their design concepts and learned how to utilize their suite of graphics and logos. They were *very* particular about their image, down to where they would allow words to be placed.

This opportunity also opened the door for us to work with larger corporations. During this time, we landed a contract with CC's Coffee House as well — not because they were looking for public relations or marketing support but because I came to the table with an offer they couldn't ignore. "This is what I can do for you," I pitched with confidence. After hearing our plans and proposal, they were open to seeing it happen. We were now able to show a portfolio of work from both Aetna and CC's Coffee House. They became pillars for us. In other words, they were our anchor clients.

Think of when a retail development center opens in a new area. They'll first look for an anchor tenant, maybe a major restaurant, to bring in the traffic. Then, they'll open a number of smaller stores around it. That's the same way it can work for your business. Land a major anchor client, someone you can work with for years, and then others of the same caliber will want to work with you as well. From here, we would venture into government contracting, which is an entirely different battlefield than the private sector, and you guessed it, that's a story for another day

Someone told me once, "You're really bold." When they said it, I knew they meant it in a condescending way. It didn't come from a place of respect but from a place that said, "Who do you think you are?" But for me, boldness doesn't mean rude or obnoxious. It means you are willing to push boundaries and trust in yourself for having the ability to speak up and take charge.

CHAPTER 13.

BEAT THE ODDS... THREE WAYS

I'm a triple threat. Except, my special abilities at the table are literal *threats*.

Young, Black, and female.

People often talk about having a double-edged sword, but I hold a triple-edged sword, beating the odds three ways.

Looking back, I realize just how young I was telling people what they needed to do. It's funny to talk about now, but the younger me walked around demanding to be at the table and feeling that there was no reason we couldn't command the largest contracts out. I didn't care how old I was. I kept a business-like attitude and focused on advancing my capabilities.

I'd often hear people say, "Sevetri is about her

business." And to be frank, being young, Black and female, that's what I wanted to make known. *I'm not here to play. I'm here to get my work done and do a good job.* Unlike the majority of young, White males, who are automatically assumed to have learned all the ropes of the industry and the know-how passed down from whomever, I didn't have that luxury, and I always felt I was working from a deficit. Because of that, I had to be serious about what I wanted to accomplish.

CREATE UNLIKELY ALLIES

Over time, I've had to be mindful that my greatest opportunity may not come from a person who looks like me. And that's okay! Most people of color go into business thinking, *I'm going to reach out to the Black person in the room. I only want to work with people who look like me.* Now, that may very well work out for you and yield great results for your business.

However.

When it comes to landing major corporate clients, it's very likely you will need White allies.

In my opinion, the strongest of these allies for Black women have been White men. It might sound crazy, but it's true. I believe every Black woman needs a White male ally. You know why? Because as unfortunate as it may be, a White male is less likely to view you as a threat. Creating what may seem to be an unlikely ally can be the one thing to take your business to the next level.

BE AUTHENTIC

One day, a friend of mine noticed that a guy, who was also a friend of ours, was jealous of me. She blurted out, "You just mad that Sevetri can still be herself amongst White people and continue to get work. Really, that's why you are mad!" The truth is that this guy felt as if he couldn't "be Black," or be authentically himself, and still get high-caliber work. That's something I never compromised on. I made my mind up from the beginning to always be myself. And guess what? I was still invited back to the table, over and over again. People couldn't really figure that out about me. They assume everyone has to have a code switch in order to obtain success outside of their Black circles. But I never played by that game. Whoever sits across from me, regardless of their status, is going to have to take me as I am and have conversations that are *real*.

There was a time I sat with a man from a large, billion-dollar corporation, and he started talking about how he's over procurement. He had recently gone to a conference and the Black people there made him feel guilty and attacked. He admitted that he (and others like him) wanted to stop going into those types of environments. And I got it. I listened to his side and let him freely express his feelings, but then, I explained why we feel and respond the way that we do. The conversation was *real* and necessary to have. It brought on a clear understanding between both of us. You see, if you're serious about building relationships and connections, you're going to have to master being authentic as well as empathetic and able to make others feel comfortable around you.

KEEP IT GOING.

Another challenge that comes along with being young, Black, and female is that you're generally challenged with getting smaller contracts. They want to give you the leftovers.

Early on, I started noticing that White-owned agencies were getting million-dollar contracts *effortlessly*. It was happening right before my eyes. They were basically being told, "Hey, we're going to give you a million dollars to start a business." (*Believe it or not, that's real life*.) Many are literally "given" contracts from their homeboys who work in the city government or friends at large corporations with huge budgets.

Once you understand that this is the case a lot of times, you can learn to get past it with your head held high. Sure, we can have a pity party, but life is *not* fair. Therefore, to win anyway, you have to keep it going. Learn to swallow whatever it is and build what I like to call a "screw these people, I'm going to get mine" mindset.

Sometimes, you may have to create opportunities as you see them and confront the issues directly. Don't be afraid to say, "No way. You are about to develop fair contracting processes, and we're going to have a conversation about how you can do that. This is what I'm bringing to the table, and this is how I'm able to diversify what you're doing."

It's important to know how to feel out a situation and not be shocked by it. Understand that everyone's a human. Everyone's dealing with their own insecurities and situations. It is what it is. *Life ain't fair*, nor can you expect business to be. You have to keep it going, and realizing this will help you get over countless hurdles and beat the odds, however you must.

They condition us to say it's not all about the money and they ride off with all the money. Damn.

CHAPTER 14.

KNOW THE GAME

You can do some good in this world and still make money. I've always been a believer of that.

Is it about the money? Yes, it's a business. It should be. You've started a business, not a hobby. When it comes to figuring out what it's going to take for me to do this and live the life that I've imagined for myself, I am very money motivated. I like to buy myself nice things, gift others with nice things, donate to areas I'm passionate about, invest in real estate, travel and more. I also want to live in a world where I don't have to think about money, and well, that takes money! On top of that, I can hear the whispers of my mother's voice say, "As a woman, never let what a man brings to the table be all that you have to eat." That has become biblical for me! It's motivated me to get up and get it. There's no sleeping on anybody's couch or asking to stay a week in someone's basement. *You* must decide on how you want to define your life and what it means to *you* to make money through your business.

You may be thinking, *It's not all about the money.* Okay, let's be clear. Did you start that business to *not* make money? Of course not. And that's okay to say! Again, if you're not making money, what you have is a passion project, not a business. You start a business to make money. Period. Therefore, the fastest way you can figure out how to make money, the better your business will be and the better you're going to feel about your business. You're in this to do what you love *and* get paid.

At the end of the day, this is a game of resiliency. This is a game of building relationships and minimizing burning bridges. This is the game of building generational wealth and legacies. This is about empowering the people around us. That's the real secret code. Those are the doors my team and I are unlocking every day. We know the game, but even more, we know why we're in it.

WHY I WROTE THIS BOOK

Last year, I decided that it would be important to start sharing as many resources for entrepreneurs as I could via my personal website. Yet, I knew that without context they would only be a bunch of downloads with little direction. I thought about adding these documents to the book but felt it would be more useful if they were actually usable downloads. Therefore, today, they can be found on my website at sevetriwilson.com.

There you will find items such as my original pricing sheet, proposals, and other resources that can be easily downloaded and used. Best of all, they will all be free. I know my team said I was nuts! I could easily charge for them, but *a lot* of people have helped me and asked for nothing in return. I want to do the same.

So, while I hope you enjoyed this easy read and

snapshot of how I started my business, it is only the foundation of the many free business tools and resources I plan to give away to entrepreneurs on an ongoing basis. Let's continue the conversation and building over at sevetriwilson.com.

ABOUT THE AUTHOR

Sevetri Wilson is a serial entrepreneur and the Founder of two companies, Solid Ground Innovations (SGI) and, most recently, Resilia, a New Orleans-based technology startup. Sevetri bootstrapped her first company, SGI, to seven figures with zero capital, and she raised over $3MM for her second company, Resilia, which launched to the public in 2016. She is the first Black woman in New Orleans to raise over $1MM in venture capital. In 2010, she was honored with the Nobel Prize for public service, the Jefferson Award and was featured in the Senate report to the White House on volunteerism in America during the Obama administration. Sevetri has been featured in Forbes, Black Enterprise, Essence, Inc., Entrepreneur, USA Today, CNN and other news outlets for her work in business and technology.

www.ingramcontent.com/pod-product-compliance
Lightning Source LLC
Chambersburg PA
CBHW071605200326
41519CB00021BB/6879